Beach Biology

Library of Congress Cataloging-in-Publication Data

Davidson, Avelyn
Beach biology / by Avelyn Davidson.
p. cm. -- (Shockwave)
Includes index.
ISBN-10: 0-531-17764-5 (lib. bdg.)
ISBN-13: 978-0-531-17764-8 (lib. bdg.)
ISBN-10: 0-531-15495-5 (pbk.)
ISBN-13: 978-0-531-15495-3 (pbk.)

1. Coastal ecology--Juvenile literature. 2. Coastal biology--Juvenile
literature. I. Title.

QH541.5.C65D38 2007
577.5'1--dc22
2007008938

Published in 2008 by Children's Press, an imprint of Scholastic Inc.,
557 Broadway, New York, New York 10012
www.scholastic.com

08 09 10 11 12 13 14 15 16 17
10 9 8 7 6 5 4 3 2 1

Printed in China through Colorcraft Ltd., Hong Kong

Author: Avelyn Davidson
Editor: Avelyn Davidson
Designer: Emma Alsweiler
Photo Researcher: Jamshed Mistry

Photographs by: ANTPhoto.com/NHPA (high and low tides, pp. 12–13); **Brand X** (p. 5; p. 24);
Getty Images (black sandy beach, p. 14; clam, p. 15; volunteers, students, newly hatched
turtles, pp. 26–27; p. 29); **More Images/NPL** (gulls, pp. 16–17; pp. 30–31); © **Paul Escourt/
New Zealand Herald** (fairy terns, p. 17); **Photolibrary** (p. 3; pp. 8–11; pink sandy beach,
pp. 14–15; oystercatchers, pp. 16–17; sea otter, p. 20; beach cleanup volunteers, pp. 28–29);
Stock.Xchng (crab, p. 13); **www.stockcentral.co.nz** (pp. 28–29); **Tranz/Corbis** (cover; p. 7;
kelp forest, octopus, pp. 20–21; egg-laying turtle, p. 27; fish farm, pp. 32–33)

All illustrations and other photographs © Weldon Owen Education Inc.

SHOCKWAVE
SCIENCE

Beach Biology

Avelyn Davidson

children's press®

An imprint of Scholastic Inc.

NEW YORK • TORONTO • LONDON • AUCKLAND • SYDNEY
MEXICO CITY • NEW DELHI • HONG KONG
DANBURY, CONNECTICUT

CHECK THESE OUT!

SHOCKER

Stuff to Shock,
Surprise, and
Amaze You

Quick Recaps
and Notable
Notes

Word Stunners
and Other Oddities

The Heads-Up
on Expert Reading

Links to More
Information

CONTENTS

biology the scientific study of living things

crustacean (*kruss TAY shun*) an animal, such as a crab, that has a hard, crust-like covering and jointed legs

environment the natural surroundings in a place, including plants and animals, landforms, bodies of water, and climate

marine to do with the sea

mollusk (*MOL uhsk*) a soft-bodied animal, such as a clam, that lacks a backbone and is usually covered by a hard outer shell

plankton tiny animals and plants that float in the ocean

tide the continual rise and fall in the level of the ocean's surface, caused by the pull of the sun and moon on Earth

· ·

For additional vocabulary, see Glossary on page 34.

The *-ology* suffix on words means "the study of." An *-ologist* ending refers to the person doing the study. So a biologist studies biology.

Horned ghost crab on beach

Biology is the study of living **organisms** in all their varied forms, in all their various **environments**. Land meets the ocean at the coastline. This meeting of land and sea produces many different **habitats**. There are coral reefs and rocky or sandy shores. There are **estuaries** with mangrove forests. There are kelp forests and sea-grass meadows.

Coastline environments are **buffeted** by the wind, waves, and currents. The plants and animals that live there are subject to the constant ebbing and flowing, or falling and rising, of **tides**. People and pollution create hazards. The organisms that live in these places have **adapted** to their unpredictable environments in many remarkable ways.

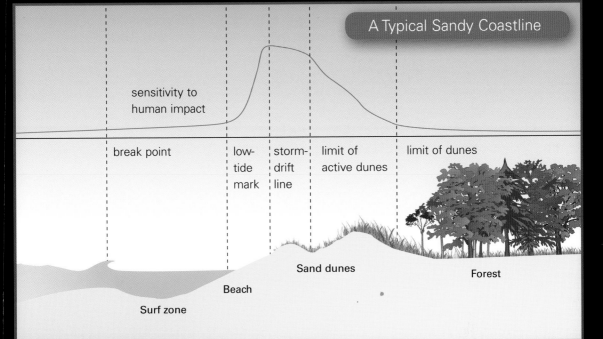

A Typical Sandy Coastline

sensitivity to human impact

break point

low-tide mark

storm-drift line

limit of active dunes

limit of dunes

Sand dunes

Forest

Beach

Surf zone

Waves and Currents

The ocean is always in motion. As soon as the wind begins to blow, the ocean responds by creating waves. The harder and longer the wind blows, the bigger the waves. Ocean waves are called swells. They can travel long distances across the oceans before breaking on our coastlines.

Currents are massive bodies of water that travel long distances around the world. Currents are like rivers in the ocean. There are seven main ocean currents and thousands of smaller ones. They move in large, circular streams at about a walking pace.

Africa

The main force that produces the ocean currents is wind. Earth's spin influences the direction of the currents. In the northern half of the world, the currents are pushed right. In the southern half, they are pushed left. Winds carry the warm and cold currents along the shorelines. They affect the climate of the various **continents** and islands on the way.

South America

Gulf Stream

Californian

Gulf Stream

Africa

North Equatorial

Equator

South Equatorial

South America

Australia

New Zealand

Easter Island

West Wind Drift

West Wind Drift

Antarctica

Bottles thrown in here

Australia

New Zealand

Antarctica

Fast Facts About Currents

- 7 main ocean currents
- move in circular streams
- produced mainly by wind
- affect the world's climate

In 1997, Nigel Wace threw 20 bottles overboard from a ship traveling between South America and Antarctica. He wanted to figure out how far and how fast ocean litter travels.

Most of the bottles took two years to drift to western Australia and nearly three years to drift to New Zealand. Others reached southern Africa and Easter Island.

Wace says that he would no longer throw any trash into the ocean, even for an experiment. This is because there is already so much litter in the ocean.

11

Tides

Oceans are also influenced by the gravitational pull of the sun and moon. This pull causes the tides. Tides are the pulse of the ocean. Each day, the ocean along our coastlines rises and then falls again. High tide and low tide occur about six hours apart. The difference in height between high tide and low tide is called the tidal height.

The force of gravity pulls one object toward another. It controls the motion of the planets in orbit around the sun. The gravitational pull of the sun and the moon on the Earth causes the tides. The oceans are pulled in different directions depending on where the sun and moon are. As the moon is much closer to Earth than the sun is, its pull is greater. When the sun and moon are pulling in the same direction, the highest high tides are caused. When the sun and moon are pulling in different directions, a slightly lower high tide occurs.

> I guess the pulse of the ocean is like my own pulse, only much slower. That idea helped me make a connection.

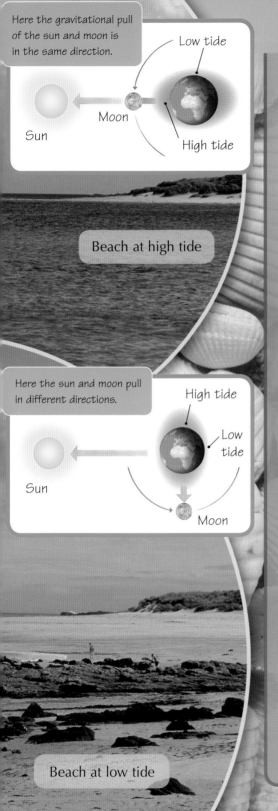

Here the gravitational pull of the sun and moon is in the same direction.

Low tide

Moon

Sun

High tide

Beach at high tide

Here the sun and moon pull in different directions.

High tide

Low tide

Sun

Moon

Beach at low tide

SPECIES SPOTLIGHT
Crab

Crabs are **crustaceans**. They are related to lobsters and shrimp. They have adaptations that allow them to live on land and in the sea. They are able to walk and run sideways, as well as burrow and swim.

Like fish, crabs use gills to breathe. They extract oxygen from the water. When crabs are out of the water, they close off their gills to keep them damp. They can live for a long time on shore if they can hide in a moist place. Many crabs seek shelter under rocks or burrow into the damp sand when the tide goes out.

13

Sandy Shores

Sandy shores make up about 75 percent of the world's ice-free coastlines. There are many different kinds of beaches. The color of sand depends on the material it is made from. It can be black, gold, white, brown, or even pink. Sandy coastlines are always changing. Sand is moved up, down, and along the shore by the force of the waves and wind. Often huge sand dunes are formed.

Sandy shorelines teem with animal life. However, most species are not visible to the naked eye. They live between the sand grains. Although small, most of these animals are very mobile. They **migrate** up and down the beach with the tides, or in response to light or temperature. Larger species of animals include **mollusks**, such as clams, and also worms, crabs, and sandhoppers. Most shellfish and crabs can quickly burrow out of sight. This protects them from predators and from the sun's heat when the tide is low.

Black beach

Sand dunes

Pink beach

Teem and *team* are homophones. Those are words that sound the same but have different spellings and meanings.

The longneck clam is a burrowing **bivalve mollusk**. It lives in sand or soft mud in shallow coastal waters. The entire clam cannot fit inside its own shell. The siphon, sometimes called a neck, hangs out. Clams are filter feeders. They feed on **plankton** through their double-tubed siphon. The siphon takes in food and gets rid of waste. Clams are a popular food when steamed, fried, or made into clam chowder.

The surf zone acts as a nursery for some kinds of fish.
Swimming prawns, shrimp, and other smaller crustaceans
and mollusks also hang out there. Larger species migrate
up and down the beach with the tides. They search
for food that the waves stir up.

Many seabirds **inhabit** sandy shores. They feed on the
creatures that live there. Gulls dive to catch small fish.
Birds such as oystercatchers crack open shellfish to eat.

SPECIES SPOTLIGHT
Fairy Tern

Conservation Ranger

- puts up signs to warn people birds are nesting
- collects and **incubates** eggs
- returns eggs when ready to hatch
- keeps watch over chicks

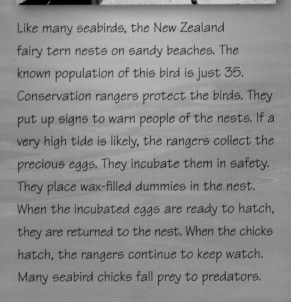

Like many seabirds, the New Zealand fairy tern nests on sandy beaches. The known population of this bird is just 35. Conservation rangers protect the birds. They put up signs to warn people of the nests. If a very high tide is likely, the rangers collect the precious eggs. They incubate them in safety. They place wax-filled dummies in the nest. When the incubated eggs are ready to hatch, they are returned to the nest. When the chicks hatch, the rangers continue to keep watch. Many seabird chicks fall prey to predators.

Oystercatchers

Chick   Adult

17

Rocky Shores

There are several kinds of rocky shorelines. Some are sheer cliffs. Others have platforms cut by the action of the waves. Many are areas that are littered with rocks and boulders.

These varied shores are rich in animal and plant life. Seaweeds and sea anemones cling to the rocks. Shellfish, such as oysters and mussels, attach themselves firmly to the rocks. Octopuses and crabs hide in rocky spots. Large fish swim around looking for smaller fish to eat.

Mussels are bivalve mollusks. They open to feed when they are covered by the tide.

Small octopuses are common in rock pools. They are shy and hide when disturbed.

Blennies hide under stones or dart from one rocky hole to the next.

Hermit crabs have soft bodies. They live in abandoned shells.

Sea stars are **carnivorous**. They move slowly on hundreds of tiny feet.

The animals and plants that live in these rocky, wave-swept places need to be able to cope with the extremes in weather. They need to be able to cope with regular high and low tides. Many have shells that they withdraw into at low tide if they are exposed on the rocks.

Life in a Tidal Rock Pool

The intertidal zone is covered by the ocean at high tide and exposed at low tide. It is the place where most people encounter marine life. A tidal pool is a study in survival and adaptation.

Seaweeds are **marine** algae. Unlike most land plants, they do not have flowers, fruit, seeds, or roots.

Inside a Sea Star

Water enters here.

Tubes pump water in.

Tube feet grip the seabed.

Sea anemones are animals, not plants. They feed on smaller animals.

Periwinkles withdraw into their shells and shut themselves in when they are out of the water.

Kelp forests grow along some rocky coastlines. Giant kelp forests are home to hundreds of sea creatures. Sea otters, fish, sea urchins, crabs, sponges, and sea squirts are just some of the creatures that live there.

These forests are an important link in ocean **food chains**. In winter, wild winds and waves may rip the kelp from the rocks, making the forest thinner. In spring, new branches grow quickly, making the kelp forest thick again. All the plants are attached to the bottom by a root-like structure called a holdfast. Some kelps have floats, or gas-filled chambers, at the base of their fronds. They help them float upright. The adult plants reproduce by spores. Thousands of these are released, but most never complete their life cycle. Those that survive grow very quickly, often growing 12 inches a day. This makes them the fastest-growing plants in the world!

1

5

Sea otter

The diagram helped me better understand how food chains work. It's interesting that a food chain always starts with a plant.

SPECIES SPOTLIGHT
Octopus

There are more than 280 species of octopus. They inhabit nearly every kind of ocean environment. Octopuses live alone. They often hide in a rocky cave or den. They eat mostly shellfish or crustaceans, such as shrimp. They leave the leftover shells and bones at their den entrance.

Octopuses are experts at camouflage. They can change the color of their skin to match their surroundings. They can also squirt ink to hide themselves while they escape.

1. Kelp soak up sunlight for **photosynthesis**. The forest grows.

2. A sea snail nibbles the kelp.

3. A lobster eats the sea snail.

4. A shark eats the lobster.

5. After the shark dies, a crab feeds on its remains.

21

River Meets Sea

Freshwater and salty water meet in an estuary. This is a gateway between a river and the ocean. Estuaries attract many kinds of life. This is because plenty of nutrients wash into them from the land. Salmon swim through them to lay their eggs in rivers before traveling back to the ocean. Fish spawn in estuaries. Newly hatched fish shelter in the beds of sea grass or mangroves that grow there.

Estuaries are important habitats. They:

- attract many kinds of life
- provide protection for young animals
- provide food for flocks of birds
- provide food for people

At low tide, flocks of birds wade on the mud flats. They are looking for crabs, worms, and shellfish. People fish in estuaries, or go there to collect shellfish at low tide.

A river sometimes breaks into several streams, called tributaries, as it reaches the sea. Mud is carried by the streams and deposited at the mouth of the river. This creates a flat lowland called a **delta**. The rich soil in deltas makes them good areas for farming.

The Life of a Mussel

Mussels begin life as tiny **larvae**. They propel themselves through the water using small, hair-like projections. As the larvae develop, they grow two shells that are hinged together at the narrow end. The developing larvae then anchor themselves to a rock. There they grow into adults.

Early larva

Developing larva

Adult mussel

Brightly colored fish and thousands of other sea creatures live in the shelter of coral reefs. Coral reefs are found in warm, shallow seas. They are built by animals called **polyps**. The polyps have soft bodies, and mouths ringed by stinging tentacles. The polyps construct thimble-shaped skeletons of limestone around themselves for protection. As the polyps grow upward, they keep splitting in two. They leave their skeletons behind them. These slowly join together to form a coral reef.

The butterfly fish has a large, eye-shaped mark on its side to confuse its predators.

The leafy sea dragon is difficult to see among the seaweed.

The Clownfish

The clownfish has a close relationship with the sea anemone. Because of its protective slimy covering, it is the only fish that does not get stung by the sea anemone's tentacles. Clownfish live in anemones and eat fish and algae leftovers. They keep the anemones clean.

The purple stonefish matches the seabed. Its spines can inject a deadly poison.

Some polyps have plant cells living in their bodies. The cells make food from water, carbon dioxide, and energy from the sun. This process is called photosynthesis. Most of the polyps' food is made by photosynthesis. However, they also catch food with their stinging tentacles.

The pipefish adapts its shape and color to match its surroundings. It sucks in tiny animals through its little mouth.

Life in a Coral Reef

Coral reefs are home to many different sea creatures. Many of these creatures use camouflage to hide from their enemies.

A red-and-white longnose hawkfish camouflages itself by darting in and out of the red coral.

The hermit crab makes its home in a disused mollusk shell. As it grows, it moves to a new shell.

Protecting the Wet World

Ocean currents respect no national boundaries. They flow across the globe, washing the shores of many countries. What people do in one ocean can affect oceans far away. One way to help protect our oceans and coastlines is to create marine reserves. In these areas, no fishing is allowed. Marine animals are protected. There are often education programs in place. Visitors can learn about marine environments and beach biology.

Seabirds need protection too. Many of them nest along coastlines. Often their numbers are reduced by predators and by human development. Seabirds also face threats at sea. Many die from being caught in drift nets. Others are poisoned through pollution, or die from being caught in oil spills. Birds are an important part of most marine **ecosystems**. Human carelessness has enormously diminished many seabird populations.

SHOCKER

Even Antarctic penguins show traces of pesticide. Nearly all seabirds have mistakenly eaten plastic trash found floating on the ocean surface.

Volunteers frequently have to remove oil from seabirds, as they are doing with this pelican.

Students learning about marine biology

SPECIES SPOTLIGHT
Sea Turtle

Sea turtles spend most of their lives at sea. They come ashore on beaches in the tropics or subtropics to lay their eggs. At certain times of the year, hundreds of turtles can be seen laying their eggs. The eggs are laid above the high-tide zone.

The eggs hatch after six to eight weeks. The young turtles immediately scurry across the sand to the ocean. Of the hundreds of babies that hatch, only a few will survive to adulthood.

The Florida Keys

Florida Keys National Marine Sanctuary protects an area of more than 3,800 square miles of submerged lands and water. It surrounds the Florida Keys, which are a chain of small, sandy islands. They form a partial barrier between the warm waters of the Gulf of Mexico and the cold Atlantic Ocean.

The habitats include coral reefs, rocky and sandy shorelines, mangrove islands, and sea-grass beds. These habitats are home to thousands of kinds of fish, mollusks, and crustaceans. Marine mammals, such as dolphins and manatees, also live there.

Many people work for the sanctuary. Marine biologists study the many different species living in the Keys. Educators work with tour and school groups. They tell them about the diverse marine life. Volunteers also play an important role. Some collect thousands of tons of trash from the many miles of coastline each year.

"Key" Workers

People	Role
marine biologists	study different species
educators	talk about diverse marine life with tour and school groups
volunteers	clean up the Keys

A marine biologist observes spiny lobsters, which are crustaceans.

Sea-grass beds are important habitats. They are nurseries for many species of fish and prawns. In parts of the Indian Ocean, they are home to the endangered mammal the dugong. In Florida, the endangered manatee, or sea cow, grazes in underwater sea-grass meadows.

Dugongs and manatees are the only **herbivorous** sea mammals. They grow large and move slowly. A manatee calf stays with its mother for years. They play together and communicate in squeaks and squeals.

In the past, humans hunted these animals for food. This has severely reduced their numbers. Marine biologists at the Florida Keys National Marine Sanctuary are working hard to save these gentle creatures.

A marine biologist feeds an orphaned manatee calf.

While many plurals are formed by adding *-s* or *-es*, *species* is one of those strange English words that have the same singular and plural. Other examples include: *sheep*, *series*, *aircraft*, and *deer*.

CAUTION

MANATEE AREA

you ever eaten salmon? It is a familiar fish on menus in Europe, North America, Japan, and other places. Once salmon was not so freely available. It was regarded as a luxury. Today, many salmon are farmed in open-net cages. They are fed fish pellets and **antibiotics**, which prevent outbreaks of disease. **Aqua farming** of salmon is becoming an issue with some **environmentalists**.

WHAT DO YOU THINK?

Do you think salmon farming is a good idea? Should we eat only wild salmon?

PRO

I've heard that fish is good for you, and that salmon is particularly good because it is an oily fish. I think it is good that more people can buy it now. Laws should be put in place to make salmon farmers keep their fish from escaping. There must be ways to prevent pollution from the pens getting into the ocean.

They believe that drug-laced fish droppings and food scraps from the pens can pollute the surrounding waters. Farmed fish escape and threaten native species. They may even spread disease. The pellets they are fed are made from small fish, such as herring and mackerel. These fish species, which are important parts of many ocean food chains, are being diminished in number. It takes two to six pounds of small wild fish to produce a pound of salmon for the table.

CON

I don't like the idea of eating something that has been raised on drugs. It also seems wasteful to kill so many other fish that we need in our oceans just so that people can have cheaper salmon. There are other fish that we can eat.

GLOSSARY

adaptation a change that a species goes through so it fits better with its environment

antibiotic a drug, such as penicillin, that kills bacteria and is used to fight disease

aqua farming an industry that raises aquatic animals in pens in the sea or in lakes for commercial purposes

bivalve having two shells. A clam is a bivalve. (A univalve mollusk, such as a snail, has a single shell.)

buffet to strike against or push repeatedly

carnivorous meat-eating

continent one of the seven large land masses on Earth. North America is a continent.

delta an area of land near a river mouth that is formed by deposits of mud, pebbles, and sand

ecosystem a community of animals and plants interacting with their environment

environmentalist a person who works to protect the environment

estuary a tidal body of water where a river meets the sea

food chain a pathway linking a plant and several animals in which each one feeds on the one before it

habitat an area where a plant or an animal lives naturally

herbivorous plant-eating

incubate to keep eggs warm until they hatch

inhabit to live in a place

larva the juvenile form of an animal that must change its shape to become an adult

migrate to move from one place to another

organism a living plant or animal

photosynthesis a chemical process by which plants make their own food

polyp a small sea animal with a tubular body and a round mouth surrounded by tentacles

Polyps

FIND OUT MORE

BOOKS

Cumming, David. *Coasts*. Steck-Vaughn, 1996.

Gunzi, Christiane. *Look Closer: Tide Pool*. Dorling Kindersley Publishing, 1998.

Layton Strom, Laura. *Built Below Sea Level: New Orleans*. Scholastic Inc., 2008.

Parker, Steve. *Seashore*. DK Children, 2004.

Potter, Jean. *Science at the Beach*. John Wiley & Sons, 1998.

Theodorou, Rod. *Along the Seashore*. Heinemann, 2000.

Thomas, Peggy. *Marine Mammal Preservation (Science of Saving)*.
  Millbrook Press, 2000.

WEB SITES

Go to the Web sites below
to learn more about coastlines.

www.epa.gov/beaches/kids

www.epa.gov/owow/estuaries/kids

www.marinebio.org

www.amnh.org/education/resources/pearls/marine/index.html

www.ology.amnh.org/marinebiology/stufftodo/index.html

INDEX

ABOUT THE AUTHOR

Avelyn Davidson lives in New Zealand. She is the author
of many fiction and nonfiction books for children. As a child,
she lived near a beach. Some of her earliest memories are
of exploring rock pools with her grandfather and learning
to identify the creatures that lived in them. Avelyn is a keen
sailor and has explored many coastlines around the world.
She likes nothing better than the smell of salt water
and seaweed.